D0765158

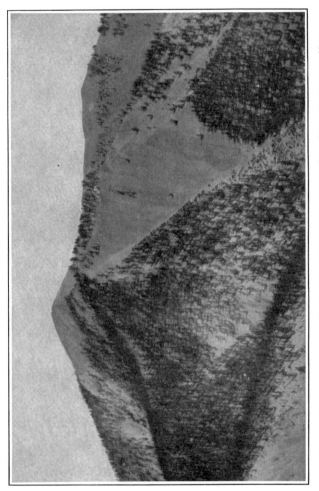

A National Forest which Regulates Water Flow, Holds the Soil, and Furnishe : Timber and Wood for Mining.

Issued June 14, 1907.

U. S. DEPARTMENT OF AGRICULTURE
FOREST SERVICE
GIFFORD PINCHOT, Forester

THE USE OF THE NATIONAL FORESTS

1907

CONTENTS.

4   CONTENTS.

ILLUSTRATIONS.

TO THE PUBLIC.

Many people do not know what National Forests are. Others may have heard much about them, but have no idea of their true purpose and use. A little misunderstanding may cause a great deal of dissatisfaction. The National Forests very closely concern all the people of the West and, indeed, of the whole country. They affect, directly or indirectly, many great business interests. It is the object of this publication to explain just what they mean, what they are for, and how to use them.

5

THE USE OF THE NATIONAL FORESTS.

WHY NATIONAL FORESTS WERE FIRST MADE.

In 1891 Congress authorized the President to establish forest reserves (now called National Forests), and President Harrison created the first one—the Yellowstone—that same year.

Congress took this action because the forests of the great mountain ranges in the West were being destroyed very rapidly by fire and reckless cutting. It was realized that unless something were done to protect them, the timber resources of the country and the many industries dependent upon the forest would be badly crippled. So the law aimed to save the timber for the use of the people, and to hold the mountain forests as great sponges to give out steady flows of water for use in the fertile valleys below.

At the start there was much opposition to the Forests. Often this opposition was just; for although Congress had set apart the lands and their resources it had made no provision for their use or their protection. The timber was simply locked up and left to burn. This mistake was remedied in 1897, when a law was passed which made it possible to use all the resources and give them suitable protection.

HOW THEY ARE MADE.

At first a great many of the National Forests were made without knowing exactly where the boundary lines should run. This was unfortunate; because some agricultural lands which should have been excluded were taken in, and a good deal of timber land which should have been included was left out. This could have been avoided by making examinations on the ground, but there was no money for the work, and so the boundaries had to be drawn very roughly.

Since 1900, however, men and money have been available for field examinations, and rough and inaccurate work has been done away with entirely. The old and carelessly made National Forests have been surveyed and mapped, and the President has put back into the public domain those lands which should not have been included. Now, before new Forests or additions to old ones are made, all the lands are examined on the ground.

The greatest care is used in this work. Every section of land is examined, mapped, and described, and the boundaries are drawn to exclude, as far as possible, everything which does not properly belong in a National Forest. Two very detailed maps are made. One shows just what is growing on the land, the other shows who owns or claims the land. Every bit of cultivated land is located and mapped, as well as the land which is suited to cultivation but which is not cultivated at present. Men trained under western conditions are employed in the work. They report very thoroughly about all matters, such as the importance of the forest to regulate the water flow, its present and future value in sup-

PLATE I.

A FOREST FIRE. THE DESTRUCTION OF NATIONAL WEALTH. MILLIONS OF DOLLARS' WORTH OF TIMBER GO UP IN SMOKE ON THE UNPROTECTED PUBLIC DOMAIN.

plying the local demand for timber, and how the creation of a National Forest would affect all the local industries of the region; especially, how it would affect the home builder.

Before any new National Forest is made it is known just why it should be made, just what effect it will have, and just where it should be located.

There are now about 145,000,000 acres of National Forests in the United States and about 5,000,000 acres more in Alaska and Porto Rico. The list in the Appendix shows where they are located and what they are called.

WHAT THEY MEAN.

One of the unfortunate things in many of the discussions about National Forests is that the facts concerning them are sometimes mistaken or misrepresented. This is because their real working is not understood. For example, a common argument used by those who oppose them is that when a National Forest is made all the resources of the region are at once locked up, industry checked, settlement prohibited, and future growth made impossible or very difficult. Since a National Forest really does none of these things, but works just the other way, it is well to have a thorough understanding of what the actual effect is.

Before a National Forest is made we have a forest-covered area of public mountain land upon which the various land laws apply. These open lands may be taken up and patented under the timber and stone act, under all the mineral laws, and possibly some of them under the homestead law, if they are suitable for culti-

vation.   Under whatever law it is taken up, the land
and all its resources pass out of the hands of the people
forever.   Consider now what happens when this open
public domain is declared a National Forest.

TO THE HOME SEEKER.

What happens to the home seeker?   When a National
Forest is created the home maker is not interfered with in
the least.   In the first place, before the Forest is created,
agricultural lands are carefully excluded from the boundaries.   It often happens, however, that there are little
patches of agricultural land so located within the boundaries that it is impossible to cut them out.   Such lands
are open to settlement.   Congress has extended the
homestead law, slightly modified, to the National Forests.   The home seeker can travel all through a Forest,
pick out the agricultural land he wants for a home, apply
for it, have it listed, settle upon it when listed, enter it,
build his home, cultivate his fields, patent it, and spend
the rest of his days there.   The only thing he must be
careful about is to obey the law and take the land for a
home, and not for other purposes.

A National Forest, then, does not in the least shut
out real settlement.   It encourages it.   The more settlers, the more men on hand to fight fires, the better
protection the Forest will get, and the better and fuller
will be the use of all its resources.

TO THE PROSPECTOR AND MINER.

What happens to prospecting and mining?   They go
on just as if there were no National Forest there.   The
prospector is absolutely free to travel about and explore

just as much as he pleases and wherever he pleases, without asking anybody's permission. When he strikes mineral he can stake out, locate, record, and develop just as many claims as he thinks are worth while, precisely as he would on the public domain. If he wants to get patent to any of them, he can do so. The only thing he must be careful about is to obey the law and not take up claims merely for the timber on them or to get possession of the land for purposes not connected with mining. Claims can be developed and turned into paying mines just as anywhere else. A National Forest does not affect this work in the least, except that it keeps timber in the country for the use of the mines when they need it and as long as they need it.

Prospecting and mining are absolutely unchecked. The resources of the National Forests must be used and the country opened up. Therefore the more mining and prospecting, the better.

TO THE USER OF TIMBER.

What happens to the timber and wood? The timber and stone act does not apply in a National Forest. The title to lands valuable chiefly for timber can not pass from the Government.

But are the timber and wood locked up? Very far from it. The timber is there to be *used*, now and in the future. It is given away, for domestic use, to the man with a home and to the prospector developing his claim. They get it for the asking, free of charge. When wanted for commercial purposes, timber is sold to the small man and to the big man—sold promptly and at a reasonable cost. The small man can buy a few thousand feet; the big man can buy many million feet, provided it is a good thing for all the people to let him purchase a large amount, but not otherwise. The local demand is always considered first. There is no chance for monopoly, because the Secretary of Agriculture must by law sell as much or as little as he thinks best, to whom and at whatever price he thinks will best serve the interests of all the people.

Thus the timber is there, first of all, to be used. The more it is used, the better. Far from being locked up, it is, on the contrary, opened up, and opened up on fair terms to all alike. When it is on the open public domain it is often very hard and sometimes impossible for the small man to get it and hold it, because he is shoved aside by the big timber corporations with which he can not compete. On National Forests the Government holds the timber with a special view to its use by the small user. At the present time nine-tenths of the timber sales on National Forests are for amounts less than $500.

In 1906 75,000,000 board feet were given away and 700,000,000 board feet were sold.

TO THE USER OF THE RANGE.

What happens to the range? Most of the timber land in the West is good range for live stock. This range has to be included in the National Forests, because it goes with the timber and can not be separated from it.

Is it shut out from use? Quite the contrary. It is grazed by cattle, sheep, and horses just as it always has been. It is one of the resources and is there to be used. At present it is used by about 1,500,000 cattle and horses

PLATE II.

Wise Use. The Land Logged with Care and Protected From Fire. The Timber and Wood Keep Coming.

and 6,000,000 sheep. The Government protects it from being burned up or from being overcrowded and overgrazed, prevents disputes between the owners of stock, and sees that each owner gets the use of that range to which he has the best right. The small man with a home in or near a National Forest always gets the first chance.

TO THE USER OF WATER.

What happens to the water? Nothing, except that the flow is steadier. The creation of a National Forest has no effect whatever on the laws which govern the appropriation of water. This is a matter governed entirely by State and Territorial laws.

TO THE OTHER USERS.

How can the land itself be used? The land itself can be used for all purposes. The main thing is that the land, as well as what grows upon it, must be used for the purpose for which it is most valuable On it may be built stores, hotels, residences, power plants, mills, and many other things. All these are advantages to National Forests, because they help to get the fullest use out of the land and its resources. Railroads, wagon roads, trails, canals, flumes, reservoirs, and telephone and power lines may be constructed whenever and wherever they are needed, as long as they do no unnecessary damage to the Forest. Improvements of this kind help to open up the country, and that is what is wanted.

TO THE TAXPAYER.

What happens to county taxes?   People who are unfamiliar with the laws about National Forests often argue that they work hardships on the counties in which they lie by withdrawing a great deal of land from taxation. They say that if the lands were left open to pass into private hands there would be much more taxable property for the support of school and road districts.   The National Government of course pays no taxes.   But it does something better.   It pays those counties in which the Forests are located 10 per cent of all the receipts from the sale of timber, use of the range, and various other uses, and it does this every year.   It is a sure and steady income, because the resources of National Forests are used in such a way that they keep coming without a break.   Congress saw that the money returns would soon be large, and it provided that the amount paid should not exceed 40 per cent of the counties' tax receipts from other sources.

Taxes from private timber lands, on the other hand, are ordinarily only temporary returns, because after the lands are logged they are usually left to burn up and become vacant and barren, quite valueless for purposes of taxation.   Thus a county which is partly covered by a National Forest is better off than one which is not. In 1906 the National Forests paid the county school and road funds over $75,000.   This amount will be almost doubled this year.

THE WHOLE RESULT.

Taking it altogether, then, it will be seen that a National Forest does not act like a wall built around the public domain, which locks up its lands and resources and stops settlement and industry. What it really does is to take the public domain, with all its resources and most of its laws, and make sure that the best possible use is made of every bit of it. And more than this, it makes these vast mountain regions a great deal more valuable, and *keeps* them a great deal more valuable, simply by using them in a careful way, with a little thought about the future.

WHAT THEY ARE FOR.

IN GENERAL.

Use.—National Forests are for use by all the people. Their resources are now used in such a common-sense way that instead of being *used up* they *keep coming*. They are for present use, for use a few years ahead, and for use a long time ahead. It is easy to draw a picture of the West, say twenty-five or fifty years from now. The picture will show a great increase in population, in the cities and in the country; it will show innumerable homes, now almost unthought of; it will show a wonderful growth in agriculture and the cultivation of vast areas now unproductive; it will show great strides in manufacturing and in all kinds of industry. This means an enormous increase in the demand upon its natural resources. Without enough wood, water, and forage it would be a very poor kind of a country. If these great resources should become scarce or hard to get, future growth and prosperity would be severely handicapped.

National Forests keep these resources coming in abundance by using them wisely at present.

Production.—The permanent wealth of a country comes from the soil. To insure permanent wealth the soil must be kept productive. Agricultural lands are managed so as to produce the most valuable crops, year after year, without a break. Forest lands also should be managed so as to produce the most valuable crops of timber and wood, year after year, without interruption. Without a plentiful, cheap, and continuous supply of wood, agriculture and all its dependent industries must suffer. And in regions of little rainfall, without a plentiful and steady flow of water for irrigation, agriculture is either impossible or unprofitable.

National Forests from their own soil produce always the greatest possible amounts and the most valuable kinds of timber, wood, and forage; and the Forests themselves make the soil of the surrounding country produce the largest and most useful agricultural crops by supplying it with a steady flow of water for irrigation and by furnishing its settlers with an abundance of timber, and wood, and forage, for home and local business use.

Homes.—Homes are of vital importance to the West, and to the whole country. A land without homes is not worth living in. What the West needs is people who come to stay. The man who skins the land and moves on does the country more harm than good. He may enrich himself and a few others for a very brief time, but he kills the land. He cares nothing for this, because he does not stay in the country, but moves on to new fields and repeats the skinning process. It is he who is the greatest enemy of the home builder.

National Forests are made, first of all, for the lasting benefit of the real home builder. They make it impossible for the land to be skinned. They benefit the man with a home and the man who seeks to build one by insuring protection and wise use of the timber and grass and by conserving the water. In considering what National Forests are for and how they affect the resources of the western mountains, the fact should never be lost sight of that they are for the home builder first, and that their resources are protected and used for his special welfare before everything else.

TO PROTECT AND GROW WOOD FOR USE.

The National Forests occupy high mountain lands, rough and rocky, and which will always be of value chiefly for the production of timber and wood. The first thing that is made sure is that the timber is not burnt up; the next, that it is used, though not used up. Before there were any National Forests enormous quantities of the people's timber on the public domain every year went up in smoke. Forests which covered districts as large as the State of Rhode Island were completely wiped out in the course of a few days. It meant losses to the people of millions and millions of dollars. Fire destroys quickly; trees grow slowly. It often takes a hundred years to make good the damage done by a single day's fire.

In National Forests there is a force of men on the ground whose business it is to look out for fire. They

33484—07——2

have been remarkably successful in keeping it down.
Since the fire patrol was started less than one-third of
1 per cent of the total area of the Forests has been
burned over, and the money loss has been insignificant.
This is a wonderful improvement over the old conditions
on the open public domain, where fires were incessant
and enormously destructive.

Hundreds of millions of feet of timber are sold from
the National Forests each year. That is why the Forest
is protected. The timber is for use. The cuttings do
not damage the Forest, because the lumbering operations
are so carefully done that the stand is left in first-class
condition for a second crop, and after that a third crop
and any number of future crops. Fire is kept out of the
cut-over lands to give the young growth a fair chance.
By wise use the timber crop is made perpetual, and its
quality is improved by encouraging a new and better
growth of the most useful kinds of trees.

The actual results on private lands where the owners
do not care what happens after they have skinned them,
are quite different. These lands are usually cut over
with the sole object of getting everything possible out of
them at one stroke. They are stripped of timber, while
the slashings which are left on the ground make good
fire traps. Very soon the whole area burns over and the
ground becomes a nonproductive waste. A glance from
a car window in Michigan, Wisconsin, or Minnesota shows
the now absolutely ruined lands which but a short time
ago produced magnificent stands of white pine. Think
of the great wealth which the people of these States
might have made permanent, simply by using the Forests
wisely.

PLATE III.

DESTRUCTIVE USE. THE LAND SKINNED, BURNED OVER, AND LEFT A BARREN WASTE.

Then, again, wood is so very essential in everyday life that it seems unwise to let it be monopolized by individuals or corporations. Actual results show that when public timber lands pass out of the Government's hands they eventually, and often very quickly, fall into the hands of big concerns, which rarely show the slightest tendency to handle them for the greatest good of the people in the long run.

On a National Forest the present and future *local* demand is always considered first. The Government tries to see that there shall always be enough timber and wood on hand for use by the home builder, the prospector, the miner, the small mill man, the stockman, and all kinds of local industries. If local needs promise to consume it all, nothing is allowed to be shipped out of the country. If it were in the hands of individual or corporate owners, it would very likely be shipped out, regardless of local needs. It would seek the best market. If it were sold locally, the users would have to pay whatever price the owner might demand, and this price might be very unfair.

This is especially important to the mining industry. All mining operations require a great deal of timber. It must be accessible, of suitable quality, fairly cheap, and always on hand. When timber for mines has to be shipped in from a distance at great expense it often makes the operations so costly as to be unprofitable. If the local supply is burned up, the mines suffer. In mining districts one of the chief objects of National Forests is to protect the timber and keep it on hand ready for use in the mines at all times.

TO KEEP THE WATER FLOW STEADY.

It should be clearly understood that in regions of heavy rainfall—for example, on the Pacific slopes in Washington, Oregon, northern California, and Alaska—National Forests are not made for the purpose of regulating the water flow for irrigation. In these localities there is plenty of water to spare. The Forests here are created and maintained to protect the timber and keep it in the people's hands for their own present and future use and to prevent the water from running off suddenly in destructive floods.

In other parts of the West, however, in all the great arid regions of the Rockies and the eastern Pacific slopes, one of the most vital reasons for making and maintaining the National Forests is to save every drop of water and to make it do the most effective work.

No one has yet proved that forests increase the rainfall to any great extent. What they do, and this no one of experience disputes, is to nurse and conserve the rain and snow after they have fallen. Water runs down a barren, hard surface with a rush, all at once. It runs down a spongy, soft surface much more slowly, little by little. A very large part of the rain and snow of the arid regions falls upon the great mountain ranges. If these were bare of soil and vegetation, the waters would rush down to the valleys below in floods. But the forest cover—the trees, brush, grass, weeds, and vegetable litter—acts like a big sponge. It soaks up the water, checks it from rushing down all at once, and brings about an even flow during the whole season.

In irrigation it is very important to have an even flow throughout the growing season, especially toward the end. That is where the trouble usually comes. As a rule the rancher has more water than he can use at the beginning of the season and not enough at the end. The flood waters in the spring can not be used; they run off and go to waste. In order to save these flood waters the Government is now constructing many great reservoirs and canals throughout the West, at enormous cost. These reservoirs store up the flood waters and hold them for use when most needed. That is precisely what the forests of the mountains do, although, of course, in a different way.

The forest cover is also very important in preventing erosion and the washing down of silt. If the slopes were bare and the soil unprotected, the waters would carry down with them great quantities of soil, gradually filling up the reservoirs and canals and causing immense damage to the great irrigation systems. The Government engineers who are building these reservoirs and canals say that their work will be unsuccessful unless the drainage basins at the headwaters of the streams are protected by National Forests.

The home builder, more than anybody else, is vitally interested in a steady flow of water for irrigation. Often his existence depends upon it.

TO KEEP THE RANGE IN GOOD CONDITION.

The use of the range by live stock enters unavoidably into the management of National Forests. All through the western mountains the range goes with the timber; it can not be separated from it. It is a great resource, and of course ought to be used. The way in which it is used has a great deal to do with the growth of young timber and the flow of water.   If it is not wasted or used up, but wisely used, it neither harms the forest growth nor has a bad effect on the water flow.   If it is over-grazed or destroyed, the young tree growth is stamped down or eaten off, and the soil is left bare and unpro-tected, to be washed down the slopes into the canals and reservoirs below.

In the use of the range National Forests work first to protect the settler and home builder.   They make sure, before everything else, that he has what range he needs for his own stock.   Before the Forests were made the settler was at the mercy of the big stockman, who often drove his herds in from a distance and completely grazed off the settler's range right at his own door.   This can not happen in a National Forest, because the man with a home is sure of the range near by for his own use, and the big men from a distance are kept away from him.

In allotting the range the small local owners are con-sidered first; then the larger local owners who have regu-larly used it; then the owners who live at a distance, but who have been regular occupants; and lastly, if there is any room left after these have been provided for, the owners of transient stock.

Special effort is being made to keep down wild animals which damage stock, and the Forest officers, when re-quested, help to enforce the State and Territorial live-stock laws.

A small fee is charged for grazing on the National Forests, because when any man gets for his own special use any property maintained for the use of the whole people, he ought to pay for it.   Most people are quite willing to pay the cost of restoring the range and keep-

PLATE IV.

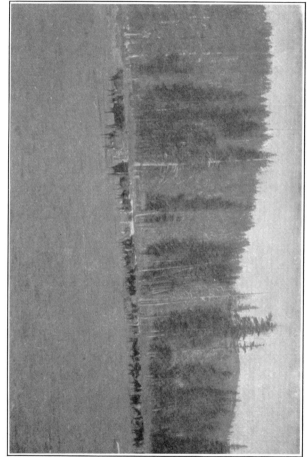

CATTLE IN A NATIONAL FOREST. THE RANGE IS PROTECTED AND WISELY USED.

ing it in good condition, especially when such control does away with the old conflicts of all kinds and assures each man of getting his rights. The men who use the range are not the kind who think they ought to get something for nothing.

National Forests, then, are not made for the special purpose of controlling the live-stock business; they are concerned with it incidentally, and help to regulate the use of the range because the people want it regulated.

TO USE WELL ALL THE LAND.

There are many other incidental uses which National Forests help to bring about and greatly assist. Of course the land itself should be put to the best use. As already mentioned, it is used as sites for all kinds of commercial enterprises, and is open to improvements such as the construction of railroads, wagon roads, trails, canals, reservoirs, and telephone and power lines. All kinds of development work are benefited by National Forests, because they make sure, so far as can be, that timber and wood are kept on hand ready for use instead of being burned up or shipped out of the country, and that the flow of water is kept even and steady for power and other purposes. The conservation (which means simply the wise use) of all the various resources of the Forests, especially of the water, means a great gain in dollars and cents to many commercial enterprises, the water-power companies in particular. The protection of the forest at the heads of streams means a prosperous life to such companies, for it assures them a steady and clear flow of water. The destruction or misuse of the Forest means failure, for it carries with it flood, silt, and drought. Here, again, it is considered that valuable rights which belong to all the people and are protected at Government expense should not be given away free of charge when they are sought for commercial use. It would seem doubly unwise to do this when the corporations which are benefited show a tendency to form great monopolies. So a reasonable charge is made for the value received. The charge is not made for the water, but for the conservation of the water.

Playgrounds.—Quite incidentally, also, the National Forests serve a good purpose as great playgrounds for the people. They are used more or less every year by campers, hunters, fishermen, and thousands of pleasure seekers from the near-by towns. They are great recreation grounds for a very large part of the people of the West, and their value in this respect is well worth considering.

Game.—The Forest officers are often appointed as State and Territorial game wardens, to protect the game under State and Territorial laws. As a consequence game is usually more abundant and better looked after within the National Forests than outside of them. Although the services of Forest officers in this respect are wholly incidental to their other work, because they are acting for the States and Territories and not as Federal officials, much good has been accomplished, and the arrangement has met with general approval. The people want the game preserved. In many cases it means a good money return to the locality concerned.

HOW TO USE THEM.

MANAGEMENT BY THE PEOPLE.

National Forests are made for and owned by the people. They should also be managed by the people. They are made, not to give the officers in charge of them a chance to work out theories, but to give the people who use them, and those who are affected by their use, a chance to work out their own best profit. This means that if National Forests are going to accomplish anything worth while the people must know all about them and must take a very active part in their management. The officers are paid by the people to act as their agents and to see that all the resources of the Forests are used in the best interest of everyone concerned. What the people as a whole want will be done. To do it it is necessary that the people carefully consider and plainly state just what they want and then take a very active part in seeing that they get it.

There are many great interests on the National Forests which sometimes conflict a little. They must all be made to fit into one another so that the machine runs smoothly as a whole. It is often necessary for one man to give way a little here, another a little there. But by giving way a little at present they both profit by it a great deal in the end. There must be hearty cooperation from everyone. National Forests are new in the United States, and the management of their vast resources is a very difficult task. Mistakes are bound to be made at first, and have been made. It is the users themselves who can be of chief assistance in doing away with bad methods.

National Forests exist to-day because the people want them. To make them accomplish the most good the people themselves must make clear how they want them run.

WHERE THE BUSINESS IS DONE.

The business of the National Forests is done on the ground. The local officers, the Supervisors and Rangers, attend to most of it. Some few of the more important matters go to Washington for final action, but everything must pass through the Supervisor's hands. He and the Rangers actually conduct the business, and users of the Forests should always deal with them directly, and should correspond with the Washington office only in cases of appeal or complaint.

The Supervisor has direct charge of all the business. His office is located at some town convenient to the users. The Rangers are his field force. They live at central points throughout the Forests and carry out the business on the ground.

PAYMENTS.

Make payments to no one but the Fiscal Agent, Forest Service, Washington, D. C., who is bonded for that purpose. Do not remit to the local officers. They can not receive payments in any form. All payments to the Fiscal Agent must be by postal money order, express money order, or national-bank draft on New York. Cash, stamps, or other forms of payment can not be accepted.

COMPLAINT AND APPEAL.

Make complaints to the local officers first. If they can not settle the matter satisfactorily, write to The Forester, Forest Service, Washington, D. C. Address to him also all other correspondence which must go to Washington.

LAND FOR A HOME.

First, select land that is really agricultural in character, then write to the Forester and ask to have the land examined and listed under the act of June 11, 1906. Be careful to describe it accurately by section, township, and range, if it is surveyed; if it is not surveyed, describe it by natural objects, such as streams, etc. It is very important to locate it just as definitely as possible. After this consult the Supervisor or nearest Ranger about how to proceed. If the applicant appears to have the best right to the land, he can get a permit from the Supervisor to occupy and cultivate it until it is opened to entry.

Do not squat or settle upon the land before it is examined and listed for entry. The law does not allow it.

Do not apply to have valuable timber lands listed. The law refers only to lands chiefly valuable for cultivation. Lands of chief value for the timber upon them will not be listed.

(See the agricultural settlement act of June 11, 1906, on page 35 of the Appendix.)

PROSPECTING AND MINING.

Proceed just as on the open public domain. National Forests do not interfere with these matters at all. Timber and wood on a patented claim may of course be cut

and disposed of in any way desired.   On a valid unpatented claim, timber and wood may be cut and used for
purposes connected with the actual development of the
claim, free of charge and without permit.   Care should
be taken, however, about the following points:

Do not cut timber or wood from an unpatented claim
for purposes of sale or for purposes not connected with
its actual development consistent with its character.

Do not use the land of an unpatented claim for improvement or construction work which *does not* tend to the
actual development of the claim consistent with its
character until you have secured a permit from the
Supervisor.

THE USE OF LAND.

To get the use of land as sites for stores, hotels, residences, and other similar purposes, or for the construction of wagon roads, trails, tramroads, canals, reservoirs,
telephone and power lines, etc., consult the Supervisor
or the nearest Ranger.   The Supervisor grants permits
for most of these special uses.   You need not fear delay.

Do not use any National Forest land for the above or
other purposes without first getting a permit (except on
a valid claim for its actual development).

TIMBER AND WOOD.

Free use.—To get the free use of timber and wood ask
the nearest Ranger for a permit.   It is given away free
to settlers, farmers, prospectors, and others for domestic
use, and to school and road districts.   It is *not* given
away free for any kind of *commercial* use.

Do not cut or remove the timber or wood until a permit

Sheep in a National Forest. All the Range is Put to its Best Use.

is obtained. In great emergencies, when you can not reach a Forest officer and when serious loss would result by waiting for one, take what is actually needed with as little damage as possible, and report to the Ranger afterwards.

Purchase.—If not over $50 worth of material is wanted, consult the nearest Ranger, who will draw up the agreement, arrange the terms of payment, designate the timber to be cut, and allow its removal as soon as payment has been made.

If over $50 worth of material is wanted, arrange the sale with the Supervisor. Consult the nearest Ranger about it and do the business through him whenever it is most convenient to do so; but Rangers can not make sales of over $50 in value; the Supervisor makes them. Most Supervisors can sell up to $500 worth of material without asking advice from Washington. Some of them can make larger sales. Under any circumstances the papers must always pass through the Supervisor's hands. He is the man to deal with. The purchaser should first locate the timber he wants to buy. After it has been cruised the Supervisor will agree with the purchaser upon the terms of sale. Cutting may begin as soon as the timber is marked for removal and payment has been made as called for.

Do not begin to cut or remove timber on any sale until permission to do so has been granted by a Forest officer.

THE USE OF THE RANGE.

To secure a permit to graze live stock on a National Forest, apply to the Supervisor. The nearest Ranger will furnish an application blank. The Supervisor

grants the permit. Every year, before the grazing
season opens, notice is given of the date on which all
applications must be in. Be sure to send your application in on time. The Supervisor or Rangers will furnish
all necessary information about the fees and other details
of the business.

No stock can be grazed without a permit, except the
few head in actual use by campers, prospectors, and
travelers; ten head of milch cows or work animals
owned by settlers living in or near a Forest, and a
reasonable number of saddle, pack, and work animals
used for caring for stock grazed under permit.

The Government limits the total number of stock to
be grazed on each National Forest. The Supervisor
allots the range among the various applicants, giving a
preference to the small near-by owner and the men who
have always used the range.

To drive stock across a Forest it is necessary to get a
permit from the nearest Ranger or the Supervisor, except
along a public road. A permit is also necessary to drive
stock across a Forest to reach private lands within it, if
the stock grazes along on the way.

Get a permit from the Supervisor before constructing
drift and pasture fences and corrals.

Remember that most of the range in the West has
been overgrazed and that in National Forests it is being
brought back into good condition. This means that the
Supervisor is often unable to grant applicants the privilege of grazing the full number of stock applied for.
It should be borne in mind, too, that all the applicants
are cut down proportionately, the big men the most. If

an applicant has a grievance which he can not settle with
the Supervisor, he may appeal directly to the Forester.

On new National Forests existing conditions will not
be changed suddenly. Owners of stock will be given
ample notice if it is necessary to make a cut, so that they
may adjust themselves to the new conditions without
financial loss.

Do not graze any stock on a National Forest without
a permit (except as noted above) or drive stock across
National Forest lands without a permit or construct
fences without a permit. The law forbids it. And to
guard the best interests of all the people the law will be
vigorously enforced.

FIRE.

The people have helped the Forest officers immensely
in preventing and fighting fire. There are not half
enough Rangers to suitably protect the Forests. The
only way to keep fire down is for everyone to take a
hand at it. Look out for small fires; they start big
ones. See that camp fires are completely out before
leaving them. Never burn brush or dangerous slashings in dry or windy weather. The time to fight fire is
right at the start. When it once has a good headway it
is often impossible to control it. As soon as fire is dis-
covered put it out if you can, and in any case notify the
nearest Forest officer at once and give him all the assistance possible.

Both State and Federal fire laws apply in National
Forests. Persons who start fires intentionally or through
carelessness will be most diligently followed up, arrested,
and prosecuted to the full extent of the law. The pen-
alties are severe.

IMPROVEMENT WORK.

Nothing will do more toward giving the National Forests the best kind of protection against fire, and nothing will help more to open up their resources for everybody's use than the construction of a great many well-built trails, roads, bridges, and telephone lines. Easy and quick communication to all parts of a Forest must be had if fire is to be kept down. The settlers, prospectors, miners, lumbermen, and stockmen profit directly from all work of this kind and can be of great assistance in pushing it through.

FOREST OFFICERS.

Most of the Forest officers in the National Forests are Supervisors, Rangers, or Guards.

The Supervisor has direct charge of a National Forest. He runs all the business upon it and is responsible for the work and the efficiency of the force under him. From training and experience he must be thoroughly familiar with western conditions. To do the work he must be sound in body, fit to endure a hard and rough outdoor life. He must be able to handle men well and deal wisely with all kinds·of people. The business requires him to have a good working knowledge of timber and lumbering, the live-stock industry, the land laws, and ordinary office work. His position is a very responsible one, for he manages a public estate worth many millions of dollars. At present Supervisors are paid from $1,500 to $3,000 a year, and are reimbursed for actual living expenses when on field duty away from their headquarters.

PLATE VI.

FOREST RANGER ROPING HIS SADDLE HORSE.

The Rangers are the men who carry out the work on the ground. They are directly under the Supervisor. They must thoroughly know the country, its conditions, and its people. They live in the Forests, often in localities far from settlement and sources of supply. The Ranger must be able to take care of himself and his horses under very trying conditions; build trails and cabins; ride all day and all night; pack, shoot, and fight fire without losing his head. He must know a good deal about the timber of the country and how to estimate it; he must be familiar with lumbering and the sawmill business, the handling of live stock, mining, and the land laws. All this requires a very vigorous constitution. It means the hardest kind of physical work from beginning to end. It is not a job for those seeking health or light outdoor work. Rangers are now paid from $900 to $1,500 a year. They have to furnish and feed their own horses. The Government builds them cabins to live in and fences pastures to keep their stock in.

The duties of Guards are similar to those of Rangers, but they are usually temporary men on duty during the summer only, to assist in fire patrol and construction work. They are paid at the rate of from $720 to $900 a year.

MEN WANTED.

The National Forests need more men. While the present salaries are too low in many cases, they are constantly being increased as funds are available. For those who like a hard active life in the open the work is ideal.

33484—07——3

The kind of men wanted are those who will do the work because they like it and will stick to it with the intention of working up in the Service. The chances to go ahead are excellent.

Supervisors and Rangers are appointed only after civil-service examinations. They must be residents of the State or Territory in which the National Forest is situated and between the ages of 21 and 40. The examinations are usually held once a year. They are very practical examinations. The life a man has led, what is his actual training and experience in rough outdoor work in the West, counts for more than anything else. Lumbermen, stockmen, cowboys, miners, and the like are the kind wanted. Forest Guards are appointed from those who have passed the ranger examination.

Information about the examinations can be obtained only from the Civil Service Commission, Washington, D. C.

Approved:

JAMES WILSON,
Secretary.

WASHINGTON, D. C., *May 2, 1907.*

APPENDIX.

AGRICULTURAL SETTLEMENT.

ACT OF JUNE 11, 1906.

The Secretary of Agriculture may, in his discretion, and he is hereby authorized, upon application or otherwise, to examine and ascertain as to the location and extent of lands within permanent or temporary forest reserves, except the following counties in the State of California: Inyo, Tulare, Kern, San Luis Obispo, Santa Barbara, Ventura, Los Angeles, San Bernardino, Orange, Riverside, and San Diego, which are chiefly valuable for agriculture, and which, in his opinion, may be occupied for agricultural purposes without injury to the forest reserves, and which are not needed for public purposes, and may list and describe the same by metes and bounds, or otherwise, and file the lists and descriptions with the Secretary of the Interior, with the request that the said lands be opened to entry in accordance with the provisions of the homestead laws and this act.

Secretary of Agriculture may list agricultural land for settlement.

Metes and bounds.

Upon the filing of any such list or description the Secretary of the Interior shall declare the said lands open to homestead settlement and entry in tracts not exceeding one hundred and sixty acres in area and not exceeding one mile in length at the expiration of sixty days from the filing of the list in the land office of the district within which the lands are located, during which period the said list or description shall be prominently posted in the land office and advertised for a period of not less than four weeks in one newspaper of general circulation published in the county in which the lands are situated: *Provided*, That any settler actually occupying and in good faith claiming such lands for agricultural purposes prior to January first, nineteen hundred and six, and who shall not have abandoned the same, and the person, if qualified to make a homestead entry, upon whose application the land proposed to be entered was examined and listed, shall, each in the order named, have a preference right of settlement and entry: *Provided further*,

Secretary of the Interior shall open such lands to settlement.

Advertisement.

Preference rights of settlement and entry.

That any entryman desiring to obtain patent to any lands described by metes and bounds entered by him **Surveys by metes and bounds.** under the provisions of this act shall, within five years of the date of making settlement, file, with the required proof of residence and cultivation, a plat and field notes of the lands entered, made by or under the direction of the United States surveyor-general, showing accurately the boundaries of such lands, which shall be distinctly marked by monuments on the ground, and by posting **Posting notices.** a copy of such plat, together with a notice of the time and place of offering proof, in a conspicuous place on the land embraced in such plat during the period prescribed by law for the publication of his notice of intention to offer proof, and that a copy of such plat and field notes shall also be kept posted in the office of the register of the land office for the land district in which such lands are situated for a like period; and further, that any agricultural lands within forest reserves may, at the discretion of the Secretary, be surveyed by metes and bounds, and **Secretary may survey by metes and bounds.** that no lands entered under the provisions of this act shall be patented under the commutation provisions of the homestead laws, but **Entries may not be commuted.** settlers, upon final proof, shall have credit for the period of their actual residence upon the lands covered by their entries.

SEC. 2. That settlers upon lands chiefly valuable for agriculture within forest reserves on January first, nineteen **Additional homestead right given to actual settlers prior to January 1, 1906.** hundred and six, who have already exercised or lost their homestead privilege, but are otherwise competent to enter lands under the homestead laws, are hereby granted an additional homestead right of entry for the purposes of this act only, and such settlers must otherwise comply with the provisions of the homestead law, and in addition thereto must pay two dollars and fifty cents per acre for lands entered under the provisions of this section, such payment to be made at the time of making final proof on such lands.

SEC. 3. That all entries under this act in the Black Hills Forest Reserve shall be subject to the quartz or lode **Quartz and lode mining laws.** mining laws of the United States, and the laws and regulations permitting the location, appropriation and use of the waters within the said forest reserves for mining, irrigation, and other purposes; and no titles acquired to agricultural land in said Black Hills Forest Reserve under this act shall vest in the patentee any riparian rights **Restriction on water rights.** to any stream or streams of flowing water within said reserve; and that such limitation of title shall be expressed in the patents for the lands covered by such entries.

SEC. 4. That no homestead settlements or entries shall be allowed in that portion of the Black Hills Forest Reserve in Lawrence and Pennington counties, in South Dakota, except to persons occupying lands therein prior to January first, nineteen hundred and six, and the provisions of this act shall apply to the said counties in said reserve only so far as is necessary to give and perfect title of such settlers or occupants to lands chiefly valuable for agriculture therein occupied or claimed by them prior to the said date, and all homestead entries under this act in said counties in said reserve shall be described by metes and bounds survey.

Lawrence and Pennington counties excepted.

Actual settlers prior to January 1, 1906, excepted.

SEC. 5. That nothing herein contained shall be held to authorize any future settlement on any lands within forest reserves until such lands have been opened to settlement as provided in this act, or to in any way impair the legal rights of any bona fide homestead settler who has or shall establish residence upon public lands prior to their inclusion within a forest reserve.

Settlement before opening is trespass.

LOCATION, DATE OF LATEST PROCLAMATION, AND AREA OF THE NATIONAL FORESTS IN THE UNITED STATES, ALASKA, AND PORTO RICO.

APRIL 1, 1907.

State or Territory.	Forest.	Date of latest proclamation.	Area.	Total.
			Acres.	
	Baboquivari..........	Nov. 5, 1906	126,720	
	Black Mesa..........	June 30, 1906	2,030,240	
	Chiricahua..........	Nov. 5, 1906	287,520	
	Grand Canyon[1]......	Aug. 8, 1906	2,257,920	
	Huachuca............	Nov. 6, 1906	314,125	
	Mount Graham......	July 22, 1902*	140,880	
Arizona	Pinal Mountains.....	Mar. 20, 1905	45,760	
	Prescott.............	Oct. 21, 1899	423,680	
	San Francisco Mountains.	Apr. 12, 1902	1,975,310	
	Santa Catalina.......	July 2, 1902	155,520	
	Santa Rita..........	Apr. 11, 1902	387,300	
	Tonto...............	Oct. 3, 1905	1,115,200	
	Tumacacori..........	Nov. 7, 1906	203,550	
				9,463,725
	Diamond Mountain..	Oct. 15, 1906	641,137	
	Klamath.............	May 6, 1905	1,896,313	
	Lassen Peak	June 2, 1905	897,115	
	Modoc..............	Nov. 29, 1904	288,218	
	Monterey	June 25, 1906	335,195	
	Pinnacles...........	July 18, 1906	14,108	
	Plumas..............	Mar. 27, 1905	579,520	
	San Bernardino......	Feb. 25, 1893*	737,120	
	San Gabriel.........	Dec. 20, 1892*	555,395	
California	San Jacinto	Feb. 14, 1907	1,751,439	
	San Luis Obispo	June 25, 1906	363,350	
	Santa Barbara	Oct. 3, 1906	1,982,100	
	Shasta..............	Sept. 24, 1906	1,523,770	
	Sierra	July 25, 1905†	5,049,934	
	Stanislaus...........	Sept. 7, 1906	1,296,800	
	Stony Creek.........	Feb. 6, 1907	883,405	
	Tahoe [2].............	Sept. 17, 1906	1,394,772	
	Trabuco Canyon	Jan. 30, 1899	109,920	
	Trinity	Apr. 26, 1905	1,243,042	
	Warner Mountains ..	Nov. 29, 1904	306,518	
				21,849,171

[1] Game preserve created in the Grand Canyon National Forest by proclamation November 28, 1906.
[2] Total of Tahoe in California and Nevada =1,453,887 acres.
* Minor modification by Executive order since date listed.
† Minor modification by act of Congress since date listed.

Location, date of latest proclamation, and area of the National Forests in the United States, Alaska, and Porto Rico—Cont'd.

State or Territory.	Forest.	Date of latest proclamation.	Area.	Total.
			Acres.	
	Battlement Mesa	June 5, 1905	797,720	
	Cochetopah	June 13, 1905	1,133,330	
	Fruita	Feb. 24, 1906	7,680	
	Gunnison	May 12, 1905	901,270	
	Holy Cross	Mar. 1, 1907	1,061,280	
	La Sal [1]	Jan. 25, 1906	29,502	
	Las Animas [2]	Mar. 1, 1907	196,140	
	Leadville	May 12, 1905	1,219,947	
Colorado	Medicine Bow [3]	Mar. 2, 1907	1,346,155	
	Montezuma	Mar. 2, 1907	1,612,146	
	Ouray	Feb. 2, 1907	273,175	
	Park Range	Mar. 1, 1907	1,133,686	
	Pikes Peak	May 12, 1905	1,681,667	
	San Isabel	June 12, 1905	321,227	
	San Juan	Mar. 2, 1907	2,203,918	
	Uncompahgre	Mar. 1, 1907	619,428	
	Wet Mountains	June 12, 1905	239,621	
	White River	May 21, 1904	970,880	
				15,748,772
	Bear River [4]	May 28, 1906	415,360	
	Big Hole [5]	Mar. 1, 1907	304,140	
	Bitter Root [6]	May 22, 1905	3,860,960	
	Cabinet [7]	Mar. 2, 1907	494,560	
	Caribou [8]	Jan. 15, 1907	733,000	
	Cassia	June 12, 1905	326,160	
	Coeur d'Alene	Nov. 6, 1906	2,331,280	
	Henrys Lake.	May 23, 1905	798,720	
	Kootenai [9]	Nov. 5, 1906	165,242	
Idaho	Lemhi	Nov. 5, 1906	1,344,800	
	Palouse	Mar. 2, 1907	194,404	
	Payette	June 3, 1905	1,460,960	
	Port Neuf	Mar. 2, 1907	99,508	
	Pocatello	Sept. 5, 1903	49,920	
	Priest River [10]	Mar. 2, 1907	815,100	
	Raft River [11]	Nov. 5, 1906	293,044	
	Salmon River	Nov. 5, 1906	1,879,680	
	Sawtooth	Nov. 6, 1906	3,340,160	
	Weiser	Mar. 2, 1907	1,126,429	
	Yellowstone [12]	Mar. 2, 1907	303,000	
				20,336,427
Kansas	Garden City	July 25, 1905	97,280	
				97,280

[1] Total of La Sal in Colorado and Utah =158,462 acres.
[2] Total of Las Animas in Colorado and New Mexico =196,620 acres.
[3] Total of Medicine Bow in Colorado and Wyoming =1,929,519 acres.
[4] Total of Bear River in Idaho and Utah=683,280 acres.
[5] Total of Big Hole in Idaho and Montana=1,917,100 acres.
[6] Total of Bitter Root in Idaho and Montana=4,552,880 acres.
[7] Total of Cabinet in Idaho and Montana= 2,060,960 acres.
[8] Total of Caribou in Idaho and Wyoming=740,740 acres.
[9] Total of Kootenai in Idaho and Montana=1,052,602 acres.
[10] Total of Priest River in Idaho and Washington=1,221,620 acres.
[11] Total of Raft River in Idaho and Utah=410,247 acres.
[12] Total of Yellowstone in Idaho, Montana, and Wyoming=8,317,880 acres.

Location, date of latest proclamation, and area of the National Forests in the United States, Alaska, and Porto Rico—Cont'd.

State or Territory.	Forest.	Date of latest proclamation.	Area.	Total.
			Acres.	
	Big Belt	Mar. 1, 1907	641,460	
	Big Hole[1]	Mar. 1, 1907	1,612,960	
	Bitter Root[2]...	May 22, 1905	691,920	
	Cabinet[3]	Mar. 2, 1907	1,566,400	
	Crazy Mountains	Aug. 10, 1906	234,760	
	Elkhorn	May 12, 1905	186,240	
	Ekalaka	Nov. 5, 1906	33,808	
	Gallatin.............	Mar. 7, 1906	888,660	
	Helena	Apr. 12, 1906	782,160	
	Hell Gate	Sept. 14, 1906	1,582,400	
	Highwood Mountains	Dec. 12, 1903	45,080	
Montana	Kootenai[4]...........	Nov. 5, 1906	887,360	
	Lewis and Clark.....	Mar. 2, 1907	5,541,180	
	Little Belt........	Feb. 15, 1907	1,053,160	
	Lolo	Nov. 6, 1906	1,211,680	
	Long Pine...........	Sept. 24, 1906	111,445	
	Little Rockies	Mar. 2, 1907	31,000	
	Madison.............	Oct. 3, 1905	958,800	
	Missoula	Nov. 6, 1906	194,430	
	Otter	Mar. 2, 1907	590,720	
	Pryor Mountains....	Nov. 6, 1906	204,320	
	Snowy Mountains....	Nov. 5, 1906	126,080	
	Yellowstone[5]	Mar. 2, 1907	1,352,240	
				20,528,263
	Dismal River.........	Apr. 16, 1902	85,123	
Nebraska	Niobrara	Apr. 16, 1902	123,779	
	North Platte.........	Mar. 10, 1906	347,170	
				556,072
	Charleston	Nov. 5, 1906	149,165	
	Independence........	Nov. 5, 1906	135,019	
Nevada........	Ruby Mountains	May 3, 1906	423,660	
	Tahoe[6]	Sept. 17, 1906	59,115	
	Toiyabe	Mar. 1, 1907	625,040	
				1,391,999
	Big Burros...........	Feb. 6, 1907	155,340	
	Gallinas........	Nov. 5, 1906	38,212	
	Gila	July 21, 1905	2,823,900	
	Jemez...............	Nov. 7, 1906	1,460,245	
	Lincoln	June 25, 1906	545,256	
	Las Animas[7]........	Mar. 1, 1907	480	
New Mexico ...	Magdalena...........	Nov. 5, 1906	146,240	
	Manzano............	Nov. 6, 1906	459,726	
	Mount Taylor........	Oct. 5, 1906	110,525	
	Pecos River	May 27, 1898*	430,880	
	Peloncillo	Nov. 5, 1906	178,977	
	San Mateo	Nov. 5, 1906	424,663	
	Taos	Nov. 7, 1906	233,200	
				7,007,644

[1] Total of Big Hole in Idaho and Montana=1,917,100 acres.
[2] Total of Bitter Root in Idaho and Montana=4,552,880 acres.
[3] Total of Cabinet in Idaho and Montana=2,060,960 acres.
[4] Total of Kootenai in Idaho and Montana=1,052,602 acres.
[5] Total of Yellowstone in Idaho, Montana, and Wyoming=8,317,880 acres.
[6] Total of Tahoe in Nevada and California=1,453,887 acres.
[7] Total of Las Animas in New Mexico and Colorado=196,620 acres.
*Minor modification by Executive order since date listed.

Location, date of latest proclamation, and area of the National Forests in the UnitedStates, Alaska, and Porto Rico—Cont'd.

State or Terri-tory.	Forest.	Date of latest proclamation.	Area.	Total.
			Acres.	
Oklahoma	Wichita[1]	May 29, 1906	60,800	60,800
Oregon	Ashland..............	Mar. 2, 1907	172,800	
	Blue Mountains......	Mar. 2, 1907	3,603,920	
	Bull Run	June 17, 1892	142,080	
	Cascade	Mar. 2, 1907	5,886,840	
	Coquille.............	Mar. 2, 1907	148,317	
	Fremont	Sept. 17, 1906	1,235,720	
	Goose Lake	Aug. 21, 1906	630,000	
	Heppner	July 18, 1906	292,176	
	Imnaha	Mar. 1, 1907	1,750,240	
	Siskiyou	Mar. 1, 1907	1,132,582	
	Tillamook	Mar. 2, 1907	175,518	
	Umpqua	Mar. 2, 1907	798,400	
	Wenaha[2]............	Mar. 1, 1907	494,942	16,463,535
South Dakota..	Black Hills[3].........	*Sept. 19, 1898†	1,163,160	
	Cave Hills...........	Mar. 5, 1904	23,360	
	Short Pine	July 22, 1905	19,040	
	Slim Buttes`........	Mar. 5, 1904	58,160	1,263,720
Utah	Aquarius	Oct. 24, 1903	639,000	
	Bear River[4].........	May 28, 1906	267,920	
	Beaver	Jan. 24, 1906	261,593	
	Dixie................	Sept. 25, 1905	465,920	
	Fillmore	May 19, 1906	399,600	
	Fish Lake...........	Jan. 22, 1906	288,800	
	Glenwood...........	Feb. 6, 1907	173,896	
	Grantsville..........	May 7, 1904	68,960	
	La Sal[5]..............	Jan. 25, 1906	128,960	
	Manti	Jan. 18, 1906	777,920	
	Monticello	Feb. 6, 1907	214.270	
	Payson	July 21, 1905	167,280	
	Raft River[6].........	Nov. 5, 1906	117,203	
	Salt Lake	May 26, 1904	95,440	
	Sevier	Jan. 17, 1906	710,920	
	Uinta[7]	Oct. 6, 1906	2,187,550	
	Vernon..............	Apr. 24, 1906	68,800	
	Wasatch	Aug. 16, 1906	85,440	7,119,472
Washington....	Colville	Mar. 1, 1907	869,520	
	Olympic	Mar. 2, 1907	1,594,560	
	Priest River[8]........	Mar. 2, 1907	406,520	
	Rainier.............	Mar. 2, 1907	2,565,760	
	Washington...	Mar. 2, 1907	6,310,740	
	Wenaha[2]	Mar. 1, 1907	318,400	12,065,500

[1] Game preserve created in the Wichita National Forest by proclamation June 2, 1905.
[2] Total of Wenaha in Oregon and Washington = 813,342 acres.
[3] Total of Black Hills in South Dakota and Wyoming = 1,209,600 acres.
[4] Total of Bear River in Utah and Idaho = 683,280 acres.
[5] Total of La Sal in Utah and Colorado = 158,462 acres.
[6] Total of Raft River in Utah and Idaho = 410,247 acres.
[7] Total of Uinta in Utah and Wyoming = 2,192,146 acres.
[8] Total of Priest River in Washington and Idaho = 1,221,620 acres.
† Minor modification by act of Congress since date listed.

Location, date of latest proclamation, and area of the National Forests in the United States, Alaska, and Porto Rico—Cont'd.

State or Territory.	Forest.	Date of latest proclamation.	Area.	Total.
			Acres.	
	Bear Lodge........ ...	Mar. 1, 1907	136,784	
	Big Horn........... .	Dec. 23, 1904	1,151,680	
	Black Hills [1]	*Sept. 19, 1898†	46,440	
	Caribou [2]	Jan. 15, 1907	7,740	
Wyoming	Crow Creek	Oct. 10, 1900*	56,320	
	Medicine Bow [3]	Mar. 2, 1907	583,364	
	Sierra Madre.........	Nov. 5, 1906	370,911	
	Uinta [4]	Oct. 6, 1906	4,596	
	Yellowstone [5]	Mar. 2, 1907	6,662,640	
				9,020,475
Total of 150 National Forests in the United States...........				142,972,855
Alaska	Afognak	Dec. 24, 1892	403,640	
	Alexander Archipelago.	Aug. 20, 1902	4,506,240	
				4,909,880
Porto Rico	Luquillo	Jan. 17, 1903	65,950	
				65,950
Grand total of 153 National Forests.........................				147,948,685

[1] Total of Black Hills in Wyoming and South Dakota = 1,209,600 acres.
[2] Total of Caribou in Wyoming and Idaho = 740,740 acres.
[3] Total of Medicine Bow in Wyoming and Colorado = 1,929,519 acres.
[4] Total of Uinta in Wyoming and Utah = 2,192,146 acres.
[5] Total of Yellowstone in Wyoming, Montana, and Idaho = 8,317,880 acres.
* Minor modification by Executive order since date listed.
† Minor modification by act of Congress since date listed.

O